To Dad
With love for a Happy Christmas

from   Sue, Richard, Sarah & Stephen

Xmas 1992

Yeovil

in old picture postcards

by
Michael J. Evans

European Library – Zaltbommel/Netherlands

Acknowledgement and grateful thanks for help go to Mrs. S.W. Rawlins, Somerset Archive and Record Service, and the Yeovil Town Council.
All of the postcards are from my own private collection.

GB   ISBN 90 288 5412 6 / CIP

INTRODUCTION

This book 'Yeovil in old picture postcards' is not a historical record of the town, as many books have already been produced about this aspect of Yeovil. This is a pictorial record of the town as featured on picture postcards produced in the early years of this century. It was a way for people to communicate with family and friends in the locality and far afield. Some of the cards were only issued in small numbers when a particular event happened, and gave details of the people and place in the message on the reverse of the card. Local photographers would be on hand with their cameras to record the event, then they would go back to their studios and produce the cards for sale that day. Most of the street scenes were printed and published by national firms and produced and distributed by local shops in large quantities.

Yeovil at the turn of the century was a busy little manufacturing town of some 12,000 inhabitants, situated in the southwest corner of Somerset, on the border of Dorset and on the north bank of the river Yeo. It had fourteen glove factories, a large butter, cheese and potted meat factory, a foundry, large engineering works, motor works, and some important printing and newspaper establishments. Yeovil has a long and interesting history, both as a market town and an industrial centre and is often referred to as 'the centre of the west'. Seeing the farmers coming to town on Monday's and Friday's, it seems hard to realise that this has gone on with unbroken regularity since before 1205.

Since the 13th century, Yeovil has been a busy market town, with market stalls set up in the 'Borough'. But with the coming of busy motor transport, the stalls were stopped in 1934. It is not difficult to imagine how the pace of life in Yeovil during the carefree early years of this century, changed abruptly with the outbreak of the 'Kaiser's War'. The names of 234 Yeovilians who lost their lives for their country are inscribed on the town's war memorial in the Borough, erected in 1921, being a cross of local ham stone in the style of the 13th century, and the town library was founded, in part, by public subscription as a tribute to their memory. This has now been replaced by a new, modern library.

By 1923 it was again possible to plan ahead, and the Council adopted a scheme for new Municipal Offices and Council Chamber (incorporating the new library) on the site between High Street and South Street, acquired many years earlier for civic purposes. The design involved the construction of the present King George Street and had the advantages of extending the shopping centre and improving traffic conditions. In April 1928 the new buildings were opened, and the land on the east side of the new street was sold to the Postmaster General for the erection of a Post Office, worthy of the town's increasing importance. At the same time, determined efforts were made to overcome the Middle Street 'bottleneck', to alleviate congestion by the provision of new car parks and to demolish old properties unfit for human habitation.

Of course, today we can see all of these improvements replaced, and King George Street now returned to pedestrian area, and the Area District Council Offices moved to the outskirts of the town. The main shopping area being Middle Street, formerly Pyt Street, still has the basis of some of the old shops. Unfortunately the George Hotel was demolished in 1962, but if you look upwards when you walk around the town, you can still see how some of the old buildings looked, at the turn of the century.

The shopping centre extends from the bottom of Middle Street to the Borough and High Street, Princes Street and

Hendford, in addition to which there are many good shops to be found just off the main streets. And now that modern day development has taken place, we have the 'Quedam' shopping centre running in parallel with Middle Street, built on what used to be Vicarage Street, also out of town shops for an expanding community.

Yeovil owes much of its success to the fact that is was a good railway centre, being served by the London and South Western and The Great Western Railways at Yeovil Town, Pen Mill and Yeovil Junction Stations, connecting to all areas of the country, passengers and goods alike.

The glove trade has been the chief industry of the town for generations and is certainly older than is generally realised. There were glovers in Queen Elizabeth I's days, with indications that the trade existed in 1361. The firms in the town dealt with raw skins through to the finished article, giving employment to many thousands of people in the factories and homes. St. Ivel cheese products were produced at the Aplin & Barrett factory in Newton Road and the Petter Oil Engines at the Nautilus works in Reckleford are sadly no longer in the town. The main existing and thriving business in the town is of course the Westland Factory, started by the Petter family with their Engine Works and Aircraft factory to produce civil and military aircraft for many years, until the dawn of the helicopter.

Today there are many smaller engineering firms in this expanding market town, to keep the many inhabitants employed. Yeovil of today has expanded far beyond the old Borough boundary and it is interesting for visitors and local people to park the car and try to envisage the old market town as it used to be.

If you enter from the west along Hendford, you still find the Hendford Manor on the right, the Manor Hotel on the left and the Three Choughs Hotel on the right. At the beginning of High Street is the Mermaid Hotel, an old coaching inn having many associations with the past. High Street leads into the Borough with the war memorial and from here Middle Street, which was the old coaching road from London to Exeter, goes down to the lower portion of the town.

Few of the old buildings remain. The Castle Hotel, once a chantry house, was demolished many years ago, as was the George Hotel. But if you look around some of the side streets, you will still find signs of the old town. Woborne's Almshouses in Bond Street date from the 15th century. At one time, at the entrance to Wine Street was a quaint old dwelling house called 'Under Bow'. Sarum House in Princes Street and the Church House are interesting buildings.

Of course at the centre of the town is the parish church of St. John the Baptist. This splendid building dates from 1380 and has a crypt which is older. The church is built of local limestone with Ham stone dressings and it consists of a chancel with vaulted crypt beneath, a nave of seven bays, aisles, transepts, south porch, organ chamber and lofty western tower with pierced parapet, containing a ring of ten bells. It is 146 feet long and 50 feet wide. The tower is 90 feet in height. The aisles being nearly the same height as the nave, give a magnificent effect, very much enhanced by the great windows.

I hope the postcards in this book, along with this introduction help to give an overall picture of what the town was like in the early part of the century, with many street scenes and a selection of the life and times in the town of Yeovil. It should bring back memories to those who have lived in Yeovil for many years, and show how it used to be for others.

1. St. John's Church. 'The Lantern of The West.' Yeovil's parish church in the heart of the town.

2. The Baptist Church in South Street was built in 1828. The Newnam Hall and schools were added in 1912.

Princes St, Yeovil.

3. Princes Street. An early street scene in 1905, with Genges Stores on the left, which
is now a Building Society Office on the corner of Westminster Street.

Princes Street. Yeovil.

4. Princes Street in 1905. This view still has some of the same buildings today. But the ivy-clad Whitby & Son's booksellers and stationers has disappeared, including the firm's own street lamps.

High Street, Yeovil.

5. At the top of High Street in 1918, the Mermaid coach is taking travellers to the station. Children pose around the three bracket gas lamp, erected on the occasion of Queen Victoria's Golden Jubilee.

High Street, Yeovil.

6. High Street in 1905. The trees on the right past the Town Hall were growing where King George Street was built in 1925.

7. A busy market day at the turn of the century. The building in the background facing High Street is the old Town Hall, destroyed by fire in 1935.

8. The Borough as it used to be in 1904. Hartree & Son, drapers, was replaced by the Midland Bank. The Medical Hall was later taken over by Boots the Chemist's.

Middle Street, Yeovil.

9. Middle Street in 1905. Even the local policeman waited for the photographer to-day. The Post Office on the left still stands today, being occupied by W.H. Smith.

10. The Castle Inn in 1905. Formerly it was the old chantry house, pulled down in the 1920's.

Post Office, Yeovil.

11. The Post Office in 1904. Everyone must have come out for the photographer that day.

12. Looking down Middle Street in 1908, there are plenty of advertising signs to guide you to the shops or local inns.

13. Middle Street, looking towards the Borough, in 1900. The George Hotel is on the left and everyone stops for the photographer.

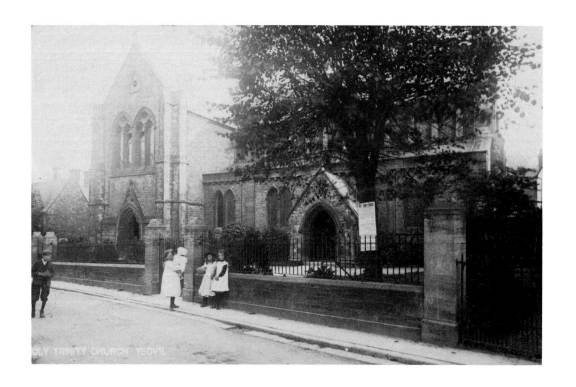

14. Holy Trinity Church in Peter Street was consecrated as the ecclesiastical parish church of Hendford in 1846.

Yeovil.

Middle Street.

W. B. Collins, Yeovil.

15. Looking back up Middle Street in 1904, we see the Covent Garden House, Seed Stores and the Albany Hotel, among many of the buildings.

16. The New Inn in 1909. This building in Middle Street, on the corner of Bond Street, still stands today and is used as a Building Society Office.

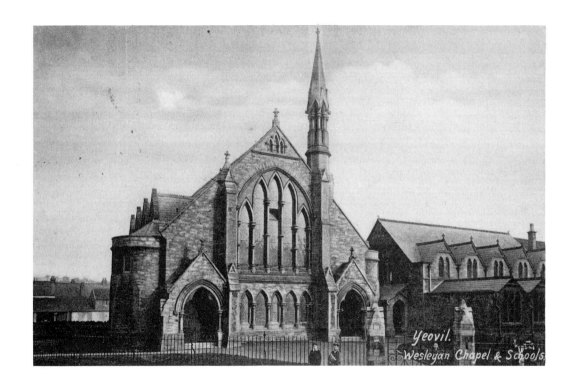

17. The Wesleyan Chapel and schools, here seen in 1904, were opened in 1870. Fire and war damage over the years has altered this view, but the church still stands at the bottom of the 'Quedam' shopping centre.

18. The lower part of Middle Street, with the Coronation Hotel on the left and Jesty & Co's large furniture store on the right, in 1906. Sadly, most of these buildings have now been demolished.

19. The Triangle in the 1920's, with the Palace Theatre and undergound toilets, remembered by many people years ago.

20. A. Ward's Palace Theatre at the turn of the century was Yeovil's first cinema, later to become the Gaumont. Now, without its decorative roof, it is used as a bingo hall.

21. Interior of the Palace Theatre in 1914. Notice
nearly everyone is wearing a hat.

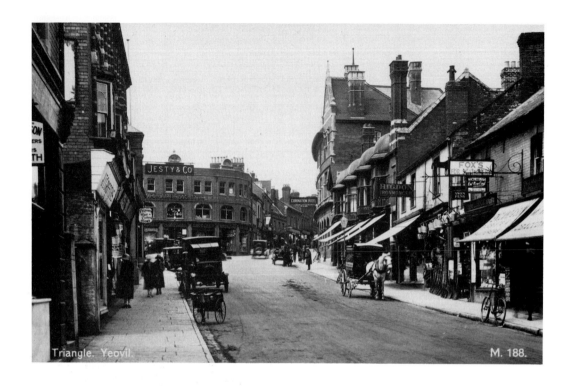

Triangle. Yeovil.   M. 188.

22. The Triangle in 1928. More motorised traffic is appearing on the streets now. Some of these old family businesses disappeared in the 1960's. The pedestrianisation of the area and modern shopping development have taken their place.

23. An early 1900's view at the bottom of Middle Street, with the local gas works, the Liberal Hall and the offices of the 'Western Chronical' newspaper.

24. Sherborne Road, with the new imposing offices and works of the 'Western Gazette', in 1906. The local newspaper started in 1863.

25. Market Street in 1905. Some of the buildings are still recognisable, although the wall and railings of the market on the right have now gone.

26. An interesting picture at the corner of Silver Street and Market Street in 1906. 'Beecham's Pill's worth a Guinea a box,' and a 'Rudge-Whitworth' cycle available from Moffat for £6-0-0. cash. This building still stands today as a restaurant.

Yeovil, Hendford.

27. The 'Three Chough's Hotel', about 1905, with the coach and staff ready for customers. 'Newtons' the chemists are on the left and are still there today.

Hendford Manor, Yeovil.

28. Hendford Manor, 1910. Ivy is covering the walls of this 18th century Manor House. Fortunately this building still stands today as a reminder of our past.

Hendford Hill, Yeovil.

29. A quiet view looking up Hendford Hill in 1906. Bradford's coal yard is on the right, leading to Hendford Station. I do not think you would pose with your pram in the road today.

30. Entrance to Lovers Lane in 1907. This is on the left hand side going up Hendford Hill, and is still in use today to get up the hill to Dorchester Road. Of course the steps have now gone.

31. Aldon House, 1911. This lovely house off the Dorchester road, set in private
grounds, had some lovely outbuildings to enjoy.

Yeovil, Nine Springs.

32. Nine Springs. One of Yeovil's famous beauty spots with its lovely thatched cottage, pulled down in 1973. The fishing lake in front of the cottage was very popular with local schoolboys.

Newton House, Yeovil.

33. Newton House: the home of the Harbin family for many generations. A lovely Jacobean building on the outskirts of the town, with the river Yeo flowing immediately in front of the house.

34. Talbot Street. A lovely street scene with fashions of the period. This street was off Stars Lane, but is now demolished and part of a car park.

35. Sherborne Road, 1906. Looking down Lyde Road, before any houses were built on the right hand side.

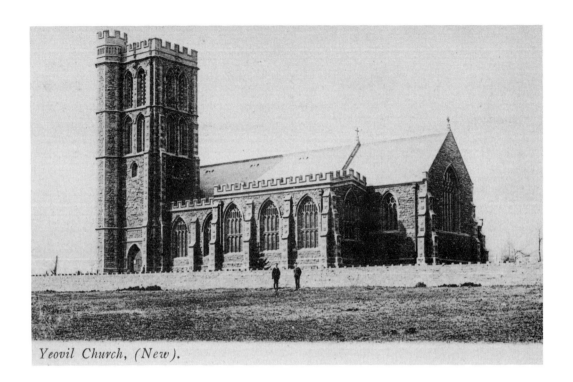

Yeovil Church, (New).

36. The Church of St. Michael and All Angels, erected in 1896. It stands here in an open space, before all of the housing and church hall that now surround it, were built.

37. Yeovil Town Station, opened in 1861. A very busy goods and passenger terminal. This was the central station of the town, for connection to all the town and country lines.

Bird's eye View, Yeovil.

38. This general view of Yeovil Town Station of 1904, shows how busy it was at the turn of the century.

Penmill Railway Cutting, Yeovil

39. A train comes through the cutting from Pen Mill Station towards Yeovil Town.
Since the demise of the line, this is now a popular walk along the river bank.

40. Friday, 8th August 1913, Pen Mill Station, railway accident. The locomotive 'City of Bath' crashed into the rear carriage of a stationary Weymouth-bound train. Three passengers were killed and eight seriously injured.

41. Yeovil Junction West. On 3rd July 1914 a signal box was destroyed when a goods train ascending the bank towards Sutton Bingham, broke a coupling and several trucks ran back, derailing at the west end of the station.

42. Sunday, 11th August 1912. The premises of 'Aplin and Barrett's', the home of 'St. Ivel' in Newton Road, were destroyed by fire.

43. A row of three cottages, ruined by fire, at the top of South Street, on 23rd February 1906. The two firemen on the roof were Priddles Hairdressers from Princes Street. And this was the first fire they attended.

MESSRS. BRAILEY, GLOVERS, YEOVIL 281

44. Messrs. Brailey, glovers, one of the many gloving firms thriving in Yeovil in the early part of the century. Gloving was one of the main industries in the town.

45. Petters advertising of the very popular oil engines in 1924. Made at the Petters Engineering Works in Reckleford.

22.

Westlands Works, Yeovil.

46. A view of Westlands Aircraft Works, with the railway in the foreground, long before all the housing and industrial development.

47. Westland Aircraft tool room staff, on 19th November 1918. This is one of the many staff photos, taken in front of a De Havilland aircraft. These were built at the Yeovil factory during the First World War.

48. Airman's escape, 1922. Here is the wreckage of a machine flown by flying officer Shaylor, which hit a tree at Newton Park, Yeovil. The pilot was thrown out and somewhat badly cut, but escaped death when his aeroplane was destroyed.

49. W. Tayler Phillips (1906), Golden Key Drapery, in High Street, opposite the Town Hall. This was one of the many stores with their own street lamps.

50. Rainbow Dye Works, No. 1. Hendford, on the corner of High Street, in 1908. It was later acquired by Denners to expand their business.

51. Pen Mill Supply Stores in St. Michael's Avenue, 1905. Plenty of supplies on offer today. Pure butter at one shilling per pound!

52. The staff of International Stores are proud to pose outside the well-stocked shop in the 1920's. This was at the top of Middle Street.

53. Yeovil's first permanent hospital. Built in 1872, this became the Maternity Hospital in 1923.

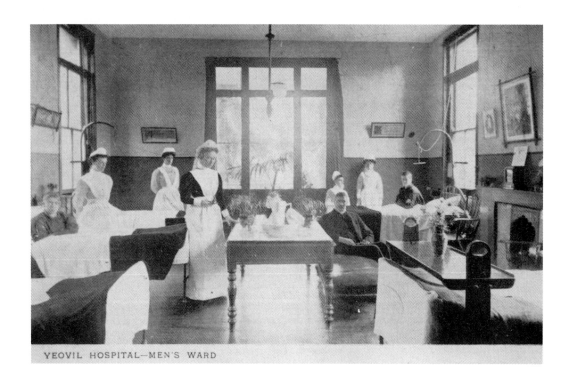

YEOVIL HOSPITAL—MEN'S WARD

54. The men's Ward in the 'Fiveways' Hospital, 1909. Matron and staff with patients.

55. The New Hospital was opened by the Prince of Wales, later Edward VIII, in 1922.

Yeovil Hospital.

M. 188.

56. The completed New Hospital in 1922. Further work was carried out to extend the hospital in the 1930's.

BIDES GARDENS (AND PRINCES STREET), YEOVIL

34270 ⓐⓥ

57. Looking out from the hospital, you had a pleasant view across Bides Gardens towards Princes Street. This early view was taken before a lot of today's premises were built.

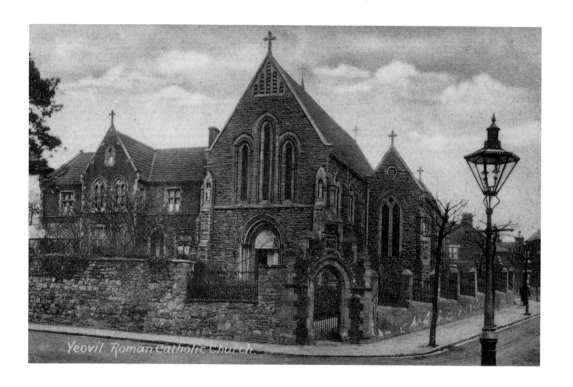

Yeovil Roman Catholic Church.

58. The Church of the Holy Ghost, on the corner of Higher Kingston and the Avenue. The church was consecrated in 1899.

59. Sydney Gardens, with the fountain in all its glory, in 1908. Note the grass being cut by horse and hand mower.

Yeovil, Sidney Gardens.

60. Another view of Sydney Gardens with the thatched bandstand, in 1908. The gardens were presented to the town in 1896 by Mayor Sydney Watts.

Park Road. Yeovil.

61. Park Road, 1906. This lovely row of old houses was demolished some years ago, like many parts of the town, for road improvements.

The County School, Yeovil.

62. The County School, Kingston, later to become Yeovil Technical School. All of these buildings were to disappear eventually for road improvements.

GIRTON HOUSE LADIES SCHOOL YEOVIL

63. Girton House Ladies' School, in 1907. This school was in Preston Road and was run by Mrs. Nosworthy.

64. Reckleford School, class ST VI, in 1903. A proud day for the pupils to have their photo taken.

65. St. Michael's Sunday School, class 2, in 1907.

YEOVIL BAND

66. Yeovil Salvation Army Band in 1905. A very proud band of musicians.

67. Yeovil Adult School Band in 1907, taken in the gardens of Penn House.

68. Yeovil Baptist Sunday School Parade, in 1907, coming up South Street. This was one of the many Sunday School parades, that everyone used to come out for.

69. The hunt meets in the Borough, in 1910. The Wilts and Dorset Bank is in the background, now Lloyds Bank.

70. Volunteers, marching down Middle Street to join Kitchener's army, led by the town band, in 1914.

71. Members of the local Territorial Force, ready for active service, outside Pen Mill Station, in 1915. The fence in the background surrounds Yeovil's first football ground.

72. Peace Day 1919. Taken at the bottom of Middle Street. The lamp post in the middle of the road has long since gone.

73. Yeovil Fire Brigade, riding on the 'Farr', Yeovil's first motor fire engine, in 1922. Everyone is enjoying the carnival atmosphere in Sherborne Road.

74. In the 1920's, one way of getting away from it all was to take a char-à-banc trip to Cheddar or Weymouth.

75. The unveiling of the war memorial to those
lost in the Great War, on 14th July 1921.

Vicarage Street Yeovil

76. Vicarage Street, looking towards St. John's Church. At the top on the right was also the church army hall. This street has now gone and we now know it as the 'Quedam' shopping centre.